D0639902

CUSTOMER SERVICE
FOR PROFESSIONALS IN HEALTH CARE:
Key Behaviors That Enhance
the Patient and Family Experience

Wendy Leebov, Ed.D.

Leebov Golde Group

Customer Service for Professionals in Health Care:
Key Behaviors That Enhance the Patient and Family Experience

Current Version: Copyright 2012; Wendy Leebov

Original Version; Copyright © 1995 by Mosby Great Performance

Reprinted by iUniverese.com; 2003

No part of this book may be reproduced or transmitted in any form or by any means, graphic, electronic, or mechanical, including photocopying, recording, taping, or by any information storage or retrieval system, without the written permission of the publisher.

Requests to the Publisher for permission should be addressed to **Wendy Leebov**; 625 Casa Loma Blvd., Unit 1406; Boynton Beach FL 33435
Fax: 215-893-3524
Email: wleebov@quality-patient-experience.com;
Phone: 215-413-1969

Keywords: Patient experience, patient satisfaction, healthcare training, service excellence, service improvement, excellent service, service quality, patient-centered care, HCAHPS, healthcare quality, leadership development, management development

About the Author

Wendy Leebov, Ed.D is a passionate advocate for creating healing environments for patients, families, and the entire healthcare team for over thirty years, Wendy Leebov has helped hospitals and medical practices enhance the patient experience. Wendy is currently President and CEO of the Leebov Golde Group. Previously, she served as Vice President and change coach for the Albert Einstein Healthcare Network in Philadelphia. A communication fanatic, Wendy has written more than ten books for health care, as well as toolkits, guides, instructional manuals, slide shows, and articles. Wendy's most recent books:

- **Wendy Leebov's Essentials for Great Personal Leadership;** AHA Press, 2008
- **Wendy Leebov's Essentials for Great Patient Experiences;** AHA Press, 2008

Wendy received her Bachelor of Arts in Sociology/Anthropology from Oberlin College and her master's and doctorate from the Harvard Graduate School of Education.

All Rights Reserved © 2012 by Wendy Leebov

ABOUT THIS BOOK

In this book, we will concentrate on your relationship with your health care customers. The focus will be largely on patients and their loved ones, although attention will also be paid to your interactions with your internal customers, including your co-workers or colleagues.

You will find suggestions for self-assessment and practice exercises that you can perform with co-workers. These exercises can help you see both sides of typical customer contact situations, sharpen your sensitivity to your customer's point of view, and understand behavioral options that will make you as effective as you can be at creating an exceptional customer experience. This is your chance to assess and strengthen your own effectiveness.

OTHER TITLES IN THIS SERIES

- **Assertiveness Skills**
- **Resolving Complaints**
- **Telephone Skills**
- **Working Together**

Customer Service

We are all customers at least some of the time. When we buy groceries, clothes, cars or furniture, we are customers of the merchants who sell those products. When we go to a physician, dentist or lawyer, we are customers of people who sell their professional services. And just about all of the time, we are customers of the electric company, the gas company, the water department and even political officials.

In every case, as customers, we expect to be treated with courtesy, honesty and respect. We expect the products and services we buy to be delivered at our convenience, in a timely fashion, and to be exactly what we thought they would be. When we have questions, we expect them to be answered accurately, quickly and respectfully. All of these qualities of product and service delivery require skill in customer service in order to keep you a satisfied, returning customer.

Generally speaking, the expectations of health care customers are not very different from what we all expect as customers in our own day-to-day business. Courtesy, honesty, respect and quick and skillful delivery of services are also what health care customers expect. But compared to other consumer settings, the health care setting is unique. We serve people who are sick and vulnerable. They usually don't want to be where they are. While other businesses can aim to make customers "happy", this is frequently impossible with our customers. The patients and families we serve are more often than not fraught with anxiety. Patients and families most appreciate us when we take steps to prevent their anxiety. And when we can't prevent it, to do everything possible to ease it. A much more powerful goal for us is to focus on anxiety reduction and extending to everyone we serve extraordinary sensitivity, compassion and care.

Why this? Why now? For years, health care organizations have been scrambling to reduce their costs by cutting back on expenses, re-engineering, bulk purchasing, continuous quality improvement, and other strategies designed to yield greater efficiency. Now, as one organization's services come to cost the same as another organization's services, service quality, not cost, has become the competitive advantage. To maintain a loyal following of patients, plan members and community leaders, health care organizations needs to excel in providing a great experience for their customers. Otherwise, their customers will choose another provider from among the many alternatives available to them.

WHO ARE YOUR CUSTOMERS AND WHAT DO THEY WANT?

Five types of customers in particular depend on you and your colleagues to deliver high quality service.
The first type, and the most obvious, *is* the person directly receiving care—*the patient (or in long-term care the resident.* Whether outpatients or inpatients, ambulatory or bedridden, your patients—their comfort and relief from anxiety —are your primary concern.
- The receivers of health care (patients, residents, members)
- The patient's family and friends
- Physicians and other referral sources
- Internal customers—your co-workers and colleagues in other organizations that interface with yours (e.g., payers, health plans and the government).

A second group of customers are the ***patient's family*** and ***friends*** who might accompany the patient to your facility, come to visit the patient, consult with you about the patient, or provide support to the patient in his or her home setting. Family members and friends, too, expect your services to be delivered with courtesy, compassion, speed, competence and professionalism. They need to see and feel your concern and to know that you want to make things convenient and comfortable for them and their loved ones. They act on their own protective instincts by scrutinizing employee behavior toward the patient and by zealously advocating patients' rights. When all goes well, and when it doesn't, they spread the word about your organization among their network of family and friends. Undoubtedly, you want this kind of free advertising to work *for you.*

A third group of customers who rely on you for service is composed of ***physicians and other people who refer business to you***. If you work in a hospital or nursing home, you probably know that people shop for doctors and doctors shop for hospitals. They advise patients about which facilities will suit them best. If you work in an outpatient setting like a medical practice, a surgi-center, imaging center, or urgi-center, you know that physicians are likely to refer people to your setting only if you provide the physician with cooperation, respect, timely results, answers to his or her questions, access to caregivers, efficient support. Physicians choose to treat their patients in and refer their patients to facilities that have a reputation for satisfying their patients and that make it easy and efficient for them to practice good medicine. Because their schedules are often tight, they rely on you for fast and courteous service as well as for cooperation and support in patient care. Also, cooperation and a mutual service orientation create a spirit of partnership and teamwork that result in excellent service.

Your fourth group of customers are your ***internal customers***. Your internal customers include your co-workers within your own setting. The physician is an internal customer of the nurse and vice versa. The receptionist is an internal customer of the maintenance worker and vice versa. Everyone interconnects to provide care or service. You are customers to each other because you have a great influence on each other's job satisfaction and ability to get your work done.

Your ***internal customers*** also include colleagues in other health care organizations who serve the same patient population you do. For instance, if you are a nurse in a nursing home, hospital or group practice, your internal customers include not only your immediate co-workers, but also people in other organizations with whom you need to collaborate in order to do your job effectively and fulfill your patient service mission. For instance, the admissions people in nursing homes and hospitals have as internal customers physicians and physicians' office staff who call to arrange patient admissions. Social workers, physicians and nurses in nursing homes, hospitals and home care agencies have as internal customers people in insurance companies and HMOs that need to approve utilization or service plans. People in drug companies have as customers physicians' offices and all settings that directly provide health care. These internal customers rely on you whether they need you to provide accurate and timely information, courtesy in response to their phone calls, or a rapid response when they have a problem related to decisions about a patient's care or treatment. This means providing easy access to quality information, quick turnaround times, and courtesy and respect in all of your interactions with these important internal customers.

All of your customers expect and deserve high-quality care, attention and caring Whether or not they are consciously aware of what constitutes high-quality service, customers almost always know when they have received it, and they certainly know when they have not.

Who Are YOUR Primary Customers?
In your everyday work, who are your most important customers and what do they expect of you? Write below your three most important customer groups and two of their key expectations of you—expectations that affect their satisfaction.

CUSTOMER GROUP	KEY EXPECTATIONS
1 _____	A. _____
_____	B. _____
2. _____	C. _____
_____	B. _____
3. _____	A. _____
_____	B. _____

WHY IS *SERVICE* SO IMPORTANT?

If customers select a health care organization based on quality, the most influential factor in their choice is service. That is what they know best. They might know a good xray from a bad one, but they do know how they feel as a result of your behavior.

Just look at the range of options available for consumers planning to buy a computer. The single factor by which consumers make their choices, assuming price and availability are similar, is service. The same is true for health care. When all technical variables are equal, consumers select health care organizations that provide top-notch care and service.

Typically, health care consumers cite service problems high among their reasons for switching from one health care provider to another — problems such as unsupportive staff behavior (coldness, impatience and annoyance, for example), service delays, impersonal behavior, and problems with their bills or insensitive handling of financial questions. People can judge service factors more easily than they can judge technical factors. So, they see service factors as a basis for their decisions among alternatives.

For patients and their loved ones, health care organizations are not usually fun places to be. Some people have compared a stay in a hospital to a stay in a hotel, or they have compared a visit to a doctor's office or outpatient center with a visit to a restaurant. But striking differences are obvious—differences that reveal why we in health care have a special responsibility to our customers to help them feel respected, appreciated, confident and secure in our hands. Here are a few of the dissimilarities:

- Hotel and restaurant guests generally want to be where they are; patients and their families generally don't want to be where they are when they need health care.
- Hotel and restaurant guests are generally in good spirits; health care consumers and their families and friends generally feel nervous, worried or even frightened.
- Hotel and restaurant guests expect hospitality; patients expect clinical expertise, technical know-how, and compassionate treatment.
- Hotel and restaurant guests expect those who serve them to be courteous, helpful and responsive; patients, nursing home residents, and visitors to medical practices expect those who serve them to be skilled, caring, responsible, responsive, gentle, efficient and a whole lot more.

Because patients and their family members and friends usually do not want to be health care customers, they rely on you to provide caring service, no matter what your particular position. Apart from the technical aspects of your job, your role in providing caring service presents special challenges and special opportunities, as well as the potential gratification unique to the helping professions.

EXCELLENT SERVICE FITS OUR MISSION

People who need hospitals and other healthcare services are typically sick, worried and, often, distressed. For many understandable reasons, health care institutions run the risk of underemphasizing the human aspects of care. People come to you concerned about their physical, emotional and economic well-being: "Am I well? Can I get through this emotionally? Can I afford this?" Excellent service is therapeutic.

For all the recent turmoil in health care and the medical professions, one fact remains unmistakably clear: Medicine and health care must remain humanistic activities. No matter how much high technology or how many machines and microchips are involved in diagnostic processes, the backbone of health care is the "laying on of hands." Experiences at the hands of doctors, nurses or other members of the health care team are intensely personal. Patients need that human touch, that caring, that compassion, and love that in itself can work miracles even when technical and professional skills can do nothing.

The more high-tech equipment and technology in a facility or service, the harder it seems to be for caregivers to remain close to their patients. Technicians stand behind computer screens, printouts offer diagnostic information, and a complex series of buzzers, beepers and other devices stand between the caregiver and the patient.

The fact is, excellent service—the quality of caring and warmth and the comforts, conveniences and personal attention offered by service-oriented caregivers—can go a long way to making both patients and staff feel human in our increasingly high-tech health care settings.

PAY THE PRICE FOR DISSATISFIED CUSTOMERS

Are you aware of the following facts?
- On average, 96 percent of your unhappy customers don't complain to you.
- However, 90 percent of your unhappy customers will not choose your organization the next time they need care.

By and large, people are not comfortable speaking about their dissatisfactions with health care organizations because they feel vulnerable and at our mercy. Their silence does not mean that they are satisfied. It just means they did not communicate their dissatisfaction to us. They think it's too much trouble to complain, they can't find an easy channel, or they think no one cares. Less than a third of the people who do not complain will return to your organization for service. They do, however, speak to their relatives, friends and neighbors.

Did you know these statistics?
- When customers are dissatisfied with service they tell 20 relatives and friends.
- When customers are satisfied they tell only five.

That means you have to satisfy four times as many people as you disappoint just to stay even in terms of public image.

And the grapevine includes a LOT more people if patients and families use

Facebook and other social media to spread the word!
The following word picture is worth a thousand examples.
It illustrates the 10-10-10 Principle:

> *It takes $10,000 to get a customer.*
> *It takes 10 seconds to lose one.*
> *It takes 10 years for the problem to go away.*

That is another reason why it is so important to do all you can to avoid upsetting patients, even by the smallest display of impatience, tension or rudeness.

Satisfied patients are also easier to serve. Dissatisfied patients take up more staff time, time that could be better spent serving more people more effectively.

Employee behavior toward customers is the most powerful marketing and customer satisfaction tool an organization has. Advertising and public relations can make promises to customers, but only employees can keep them. The quality of the customer's experience inside your facility is what makes or breaks your organization's reputation and success. And that experience consists of thousands of crucial moments —brief but nonetheless pivotal interactions or "moments of truth"— between you and patients, family members and other customers.

Your Moments of Truth
See if you can name five specific interaction moments between you and your customers—interaction moments that have a great impact on your customers' satisfaction with your service.

1. _____
2. _____
3. _____
4. _____
5. _____

RAPID CHANGE AND HEAVY WORKLOADS MAKE IT THAT MUCH HARDER!

People who entered health care professions because they thought they would be "secure" are now overwhelmed with anxiety and the disappointment of broken promises—at the same time that they are being pushed to work even harder. Change has brought uncertainty about the future of the health care industry; uncertainty breeds fear. Mergers and acquisitions, partnerships and alliances, re-engineering and restructuring, intense competition, and the prospects of health care reform have created a very tense atmosphere. Add to these the challenges of heavy workloads, multi priorities and working with increasingly demanding consumers and the challenge is clear: Provide high-quality care and caring in the face of extreme pressure. The reputation of your organization and your professional self-esteem rest on making your patients' needs your paramount responsibility, and on not letting yourself and your co-workers become self-absorbed or beaten down by the pressures and demands of these difficult, changing times.

GIVING CUSTOMERS NO LESS THAN 100 PERCENT!

You may think you are already very effective with customers, and you probably are. But it does not take much to create dissatisfaction. One instance of rudeness and impatience can become a very significant part of a patient's experience and overall impression of you and your organization. After all, patients don't know you well enough to understand that this one unpleasant incident may not be typical of your behavior. The challenge is to become consistently positive in your interactions with your customers.

Customers do not handle our excuses very well, and is it any wonder? Consider what would happen if some other service industries delivered 99 percent of the time, a mere 1 percent below perfect:

- Homes would be without electricity, heat, water and telephone service about 15 minutes every day.
- Every page of the telephone directory would contain about four wrong numbers.
- Traffic lights would be ineffective almost two hours per week.
- Pharmacies would incorrectly fill thousands of prescriptions every day.

Imagine the confusion, inconvenience and even danger that would result if the performance of these services was routinely less than 100 percent! We certainly count on other industries to deliver top-level service all of the time, and our customers expect no less from us.

Change and Its Effects on Your Customer Orientation

What changes are happening in or around your organization? And what are the greatest pressures?

_____

_____

_____

_____

What can you do to keep your focus on your customers, instead of on your own anxieties about adapting to the changes and handling the pressure?

_____

_____

_____

_____

WHERE DO WE START?

Self-awareness and key skills are needed for successful public contact and caring service. Starting with self-awareness, you need a solid understanding of:

- Your role in public contact situations and how far your responsibility and authority extend.
- Your own feelings, attitudes and beliefs and how these affect your relationships with your customers and coworkers.
- Your nonverbal behavior---personal mannerisms, tone of voice, style of dress and so forth, and how these affect people's responses to you and how you respond to them.
- Your tendencies to act ineffectively or effectively in response to different kinds of people with different backgrounds, personalities and problems.

To be effective with the people you serve, you need to accept the fact that, no matter how you feel on a given day, you have a public responsibility. Your behavior has an effect on the satisfaction of your customers, and you have a responsibility as a professional to do all you can to serve your customers with caring service no matter how you feel.

WHAT DO PATIENTS AND FAMILIES WANT?

DO YOU "KNOW THYSELF"				
How aware do you feel about each of the following elements key to successful public contact?				

	UNAWARE			KEENLY AWARE
1. How aware are you of how much authority and responsibility you have as a service-provider?	1	2	3	4
2. How aware do you feel of your attitudes, feelings and beliefs and how these affect your relationships with customers?	1	2	3	4
3. How aware are you of your personal mannerisms, tone of voice, and style of dress and how these affect customers' responses to you?	1	2	3	4
4. How aware are you of your typical patterns of responding to people with courtesy and respect regardless of their history, culture, personal mannerisms and personality?	1	2	3	4
Based on your self assessment, what goals do you have for improving your awareness in ways that will help your effectiveness in satisfying the people you serve?				
_____ _____ _____ _____ _____ _____ _____				

In any consumer-oriented business, customers hold certain expectations about the treatment they will receive. They may not always be able to express their expectations, and they may not even be consciously aware of what they are. But when their expectations are not met, customers feel dissatisfied.

What do patients and families want? After listening to descriptions of the wants and needs of customers in health care, The Einstein Consulting Group, a nationally recognized leader in health care customer service, developed 16 house rules for health care customer service. These rules spell out key behaviors and attitudes that matter to patients and families. They are not new or profound. They merely clarify what your customers want. Certainly, most health care employees meet most of these expectations most of the time, but the challenge is to become more skilled and consistent in your everyday habits and routines.

As you read the house rules, think of yourself as a patient who is being served by a health care organization, perhaps for the first time. You would probably feel somewhat anxious about the unfamiliar surroundings, and you might feel uncomfortable about meeting the physicians or other health care workers responsible for your treatment or care. You might also feel very concerned about any tests, examinations or procedures that might be needed, as well as their consequences for you and your family.

When you think about the anxiety and concern felt by the patient, and the stress and strain felt by your co-workers in their very demanding professions, the importance of positive interactions and consistent practice of the 16 House Rules becomes apparent. You play a powerful role in making your customers' experiences with you and your organization as pleasant, humane and positive as they can be.

The 16 House Rules

By following the 16 House Rules, you can rest assured that you are providing excellent customer service.

We will go over each rule in detail later, but let's start with a list of the basics:
1. **Break the ice.** Make eye contact, smile, say hello, introduce yourself, call people by name, and extend a few words of concern.
2. **Notice when someone looks confused.** Stop and lend a hand.
3. **Take time for courtesy and consideration.** Kind words and polite gestures make people feel special.

4. **Keep people informed**. Explain what you are doing and what people can expect. People are always less anxious when they know what is happening. Communicate.
5. **Anticipate needs**. You will often know what people want before they have to ask. Don't wait. Act.
6. **Respect people's time and respond quickly**. When patients are worried or sick every minute seems like an hour. When co-workers need information or help they find delays frustrating.
7. **Maintain privacy and confidentiality**. Knock as you enter a patient's room. Watch what you say and where you say it. Protect personal information.
8. **Handle with care**. Slow down. Imagine that you are on the receiving end.
9. **Maintain dignity**. Give choices in interactions with patients. Close curtains to provide privacy. That patient could be your child, your partner, your parent or your friend.
10. **Take the initiative**. Just because something is "not your job" doesn't mean you can't help or find someone who can.
11. **Treat patients as adults**. Your words and tone should show respect and consideration.
12. **Listen and act**. When people complain, do not blame others or make excuses. Hear them out and do all you can to respond to the problem and make things right.
13. **Help each other**. When you help your co-workers, you help patients too.
14. **Keep it quiet**. Noise annoys! It also shows a lack of consideration and concern for patients.
15. **Apply telephone skills**. When you are on the telephone, your organization's reputation is on the line. Sound pleasant. Be helpful. Listen with understanding.
16. **Look the part**. Professional dress and demeanor build people's confidence in all of us.

Those are the 16 House Rules. Now, to become better acquainted with them, let's take each one individually and examine specific ways you can put them into practice.

RULE 1: BREAK THE ICE

Make eye contact, smile, say hello, introduce yourself, call people by name, and extend a few words of concern.

In a world as busy and crowded as ours is, it's easy for people to feel invisible and overlooked. Especially in health care settings, where customers are often anxious and frightened, it's important to make customers feel welcomed and acknowledged immediately and in a friendly manner, to let them know who you are, and to offer them kind words and words that give them confidence in your ability to help them. Excellence in meeting and greeting people creates an atmosphere of warmth, welcome and professionalism. Even though we learned as children not to talk to strangers, in our organizations we want to make people feel welcome, not like strangers at all. Even if the person you see in the hallway or in the waiting room is not your patient, take a moment to smile, say hello, and make a warm and friendly comment. Here are examples of greetings suited to different situations:

- In an elevator, "Hello, welcome to Community General. I'm Mark Perkins. Cold enough for you out there?"
- In a medical practice waiting room, "Good morning. My name is Carol Smith. I work in Billing. And your name is...?"
- Seeing a family member during a home care visit, "Good morning. I'm Helene Robinson from Community Home Health. It's nice to see you... And how's your mom doing?"
- At reception, "Hello, I'm Manny Johnson. Am I right that you're Ben Marks? Great, welcome. If my records are right, this is your first time here! We have a great team and I think you'll be very pleased with our services."
- Passing a patient in a hospital hallway, "My, that's a pretty robe you're wearing."
- Nursing home vending area, "Hello again, Mr. Jones. It's nice to see you visit your mother. I'm sure she must appreciate it very much."

Develop a *greeting protocol* that will help to break the ice with your customers and give them immediate confidence that they are in good hands when they meet you. If you develop a protocol or script for yourself, you will not have to *think* every time you are in a position to greet another customer.
Your protocol, which you will have designed to be excellent, will become habit!

Research on what customers in health care settings like suggests these elements for an excellent greeting protocol:

- Acknowledge each customer immediately with a smile and nod.
- Make eye contact and greet with a warm "Hello" or "Good morning."
- Introduce yourself by name, explain your function, and offer to help.
- When possible, refer to the customer by name, referring to the customer with his or her title—Dr., Mr., Ms., Miss or Mrs.—unless invited to do otherwise. Or, if you're not sure, ask, "Is that Ms.?" and call the customer what he or she prefers.

Your Ideal Greeting
Jot down below a script for a great greeting you could give to your customers in each of the following situations:

*On the phone-*_____
_____
_____

*In a hallway to strangers-*_____
_____
_____

*To people who come to see you-*_____
_____
_____

Once you ensure that your initial greeting is great, ask yourself if you can proceed to break the ice in the customer's interaction with the next person they meet. For instance, if you do what you need to do for the customer and then must hand off or pass along that customer to a co-worker, you have yet another opportunity to break the ice. You can ease the customer's transition from you to your co-worker by saying, for instance, "Hi James! Mrs. Hangley, this is James Milton, one of our terrific technologists. He'll show you to the changing area."

Ice-breaking can happen almost anywhere. When you are riding the elevator, you might smile and comment to others on the weather instead of staring at the floor or ceiling. Offer to push the floor buttons for people as they enter the elevator. It helps them to feel welcome and at home. It makes your organization a friendly place, a place where even a perfect stranger is warm and helpful.

Being really good at breaking the ice with customers requires that you also be good at making small talk. This is not easy; certainly, not all of us are masters of small talk, and not everyone enjoys it. But it can certainly personalize and enhance interactions with customers and result in a much more positive experience for them. The exercise that follows will give you the opportunity to practice.

Initiating Small Talk

Below, list as quickly as you can brief small-talk "starters"(conversational leads you can use to break the ice with patients you meet in the course of your work). Here are a few examples:

- **"Wasn't that a terrible storm we had the other day?"**
- **"What do you think of the food here so far?"**
- **"Can I get you a magazine while you're waiting?"**

_____

_____

_____

_____

_____

After you've compiled your list, try out your small-talk starters on a co-worker.

You may feel awkward at first in breaking the ice with your customers, but you will find that small talk is a skill that improves and becomes more natural with practice. And the rewards of striking up a conversation and helping people feel at home will make you want to do it all the more!

RULE 2: NOTICE WHEN SOMEONE LOOKS CONFUSED AND STOP TO HELP

It's not enough just to notice. When someone looks confused, stop and lend a hand.

All too often, when customers look lost or act as though they do not know what they are expected to do next, employees walk by and pretend not to notice. Such an attitude detracts greatly from good customer service. People remember when they felt ignored in a moment of need.

Put yourself in the patient's position, and remember the instances when you might have felt or looked confused in a health care facility, especially a large one. Was it difficult, for example, to find the coffee shop? Would you have known how to find the radiology department as opposed to radiation therapy? Or the visitor elevators? Or the cafeteria? Or the patient tower, not the maternity wing? If your organization consists of several buildings connected by tunnels, would you, as a first-time visitor, have known which route to take to get where you were going?

Frequently, customers are too shy to ask for help when they do not know their way, especially when they are new to an organization. It is not difficult to spot someone who is lost, and it becomes a memorable gesture of kindness when someone who does know the way steps in to help. You might say something like:

- "Hi, I'm Sam Stargell. I work in the mail room. Can I help you find your way?"
- "I'm on my way there myself. Why don't you walk along with me? This can be quite a confusing place."
- "Let me show you part of the way. Then I'll be able to give you directions that will be easier to follow."

The following exercise will help you practice applying rule 2 in helping people find their way.

Helping People to Find Their Way

Ask yourself, when people in the halls look lost, what are at least five ways that you could help them find their way? Ideally, you would take them where they're going, and that is probably what you do when you can spare the time. But what other options do you have? List them below: Then discuss them with a co-worker and consciously draw from among these options the next time you see a lost visitor out of the corner of your eye. (A list of suggested options follows.)

_____

_____

_____

_____

_____

_____

Some of the options you could have listed for the preceding exercise include:

1. Walk the visitor part of the way; point out the rest of the way.

2. Ask a co-worker going in the same direction to show the way.

3. Ask a security guard for help.

4. Call the location where the visitor is heading. Ask whether they could send someone part way to meet the visitor.

5. Ask your public relations department to provide a map that you can use for giving directions.

6. Explain the directions. Then take a moment to write them out if they are complicated.

7. Walk the visitor to a directional map hung in the hallway. Show him or her the way on the map. Ask whether the visitor has any questions.

8. Walk the visitor where he or she is going, sympathizing with the difficulty in finding one's way in a large, bustling hospital.

Finding one's way from place to place is not the only thing that breeds confusion. Patients also feel confusion about what will happen to them. Few people who visit an admissions office, outpatient center, physician's office, or the cashier for the first time will know what to expect. You can relieve customers' confusion and put them at ease by telling them, for example, that they will be expected to fill out forms and that they probably will have to wait a certain length of time. For example, you might say:

- "Have a seat, Mrs. Gordon. Before we begin, would you please help me fill out these insurance forms?"

- "The doctor will be with you in about 15 minutes, Mr. Harris."

- "I have a few questions for you. Then one of our escorts will show you to your room."

- "Mrs. Harris, I realize this is your first time having the help of a home health professional. Let me explain what I'll be able to do for you while I'm here.

Think About Your Key Customers
What is there in your service that tends to confuse person after person?

_____

_____

_____

How do you know when the person is confused? What signs and symptoms do you see?

_____

_____

_____

What can you do or say to solve the person's confusion even if he or she hasn't been able to express it to you in words?

_____

_____

_____

RULE 3: TAKE TIME FOR COURTESY AND CONSIDERATION

Kind words and polite gestures make people feel special. There is no substitute for courtesy and politeness. "Please," "Thank you," and "I'm sorry for the inconvenience" are words that go a long way in building customer confidence and making customers feel respected. Such words show that you care about other people, that you care that they are treated well, and that you respect them as individuals. Customers remember someone who took the time to be kind and courteous.

It helps to keep in mind that what you are asking the patient to do is for your convenience as well as their care—you need the insurance forms filled out, you need to record the patient's medical history—and you should openly acknowledge and appreciate their cooperation. For example, "May I please ask you to sign this form? Thank you."

Courtesy and consideration are also critical if you want the respect and cooperation of your internal customers, including your co-workers and people from other health care-related organizations with whom you need to interact. Sometimes, in the daily rush of too much to do and a hectic pace, it's easy to suspend the thank-yous and take each other for granted. When this happens you miss the opportunity to make your co-worker relationships more harmonious, show respect for the individuals with whom you work, and add a human element to an otherwise "all work, no play" day.

There are undoubtedly many times in the course of the day when you rely on your customers and co-workers to cooperate with you. If you thank them for every way they cooperate, they will be impressed and even more generous in their cooperation in the future. For instance, you might say:

To a customer:
- "Mrs. Harkins, thanks for taking the care to fill out all the details that we require on that form."
- "Mr. Billston, thank you for waiting."
- "Ms. Hooper, thank you for pointing out this error. I really appreciate it."

To a co-worker:
- "Bill, thanks for filling in for me when I got overwhelmed with calls."
- "Would you please register the next patient while I untangle this bill? Thank you."
- "Thank you for meeting that tough deadline!"
- "Thank you for bailing me out of that tough situation."

What Can You Thank People For?

Ask yourself in which situations during your typical day do you rely on your customers' cooperation? List these situations below and jot down a thank-you statement you could use to really make them feel appreciated.

SITUATION	HOW I CAN SAY THANKS
1.	
2.	
3.	
4.	
5.	
6.	

RULE 4: KEEP PEOPLE INFORMED

Explain what you are doing and what people can expect. People are less anxious when they know what is happening. Communicate.

As mentioned earlier, patients do not generally use health care services expecting to have a good time. More often than not, they are anxious and frightened, and some even fear the worst. All too often, what will happen to them seems like a big, sinister mystery. The fact is that most patients have plenty of questions. For example: "Will it hurt?" "What will you do?" "Just how bad off am I?" "Is this going to cost me a whole lot?" "Will I need tests?" "Will I have to wait long for the doctor?" "When can I get my TV fixed?" "Can I eat before the test?"

Often, patients do not bring up their questions because they do not want to appear stupid or they do not want to bother us. But patients need to know what to expect, and, whenever possible, you should anticipate their concerns and tell them. For example, you might say:

- "There are several steps in this kind of test. Let me describe them to you so you'll know what I'm doing."

- "You can expect some swelling and soreness from this procedure. Some people also report light-headedness and a slight headache. Don't be alarmed if you experience this, but if it becomes too uncomfortable, please call us."

- "I'm going to ask our chief pharmacist about whether you can take this medication along with everything else you're taking. I shouldn't be gone more than about 10 minutes."

- "We're waiting for the results from your lab tests. Sometimes they take a few days. I'll be in touch as soon as they come in."

- "I've taken a look at your air conditioner and I see the problem. I need to locate some new parts, and it will take me about two hours to secure them. Then I'll be back, and it will take me about a half hour to install the parts. I'll be back. You can count on it. And I'm sorry we've inconvenienced you."

- "I'd like to apologize for that long wait. We're committed to giving every patient all the time he or she needs, and some of our patients today needed more than the time we allotted to them. I'm really sorry you've had to wait, but I'll assure you that you'll get the time you need, too."

- "Well, I've certainly bombarded you with a lot of information. Please feel free to ask me questions at any time."

Helping patients, families, physicians and co-workers know what to expect and what is being done on their behalf lessens their anxiety. It also lets people know that you care about their needs, want to help them, and respect their need to know.

Ideally, you will develop *explanation protocols*—standardized ways to explain effectively the things you tell patient after patient, day after day. By devoting time to developing protocols, you can design excellent explanations and use them repeatedly, without needing to think of them out of the blue every time the situation presents itself.

Here are some guidelines for developing an explanation protocol for situations where you need to explain things to your customers face-to-face.

1. **INVESTIGATE. Find out specifically what customers need to know and why; find out what they already know.**

2. **EXPLAIN.**
    - If it can be simple and short, simple tell them what they need to know.
    - If the explanation must be longer or more complex, give an overview. Tell them what you'll tell them before you

tell them, so they can prepare their minds for the detailed explanation to come. Then give the details.
- Finish by reviewing the main points.

3. **CHECK BACK FOR UNDERSTANDING.**
- Find out what's unclear, making it easy for people to ask questions. Example: "I realize this can be a lot to grasp at once. Is there any way I've confused you?" Or "I deal with this all the time. I know it's complex and I'm not always as clear as I'd like to be. Do you have any questions? Is anything unclear?"
- For long explanations, check back along the way. Don't wait until the end.
- Watch for nonverbal cues that signal inattention or confusion-looking away, fidgeting, a blank stare, a wrinkled brow. If you notice these, invite feedback. Example: "You look confused. Have I left anything unclear?"

4. **ANSWER "NOW WHAT?"**
- Identify the next steps: what they can expect, what you'll do, what others will do, what they need to do and when.
- Reinforce the explanation with something they can take with them (appointment card, checklist, pamphlet, directions, map, video).
- Consider follow up. Does the customer need more information at another time? If so, tell him or her how you'll follow up and when. Then follow up as promised.

1. **OPEN THE DOOR TO FURTHER COMMUNICATION.** In case customers have questions later, encourage them to contact you or another appropriate person and tell them how they can do so easily. Example: "Please don't hesitate to call me any time; here's my number."

2. **SHOW YOU CARE.**
- "Hope your surgery goes well."
- "Hope this isn't too much trouble. I really appreciate your getting me this information."
- "It was good to see you/talk to you (again)."

- "Good luck to your mother/wife/etc."
- "Thank you."

Helping to Keep People Informed
Think about your job. No doubt, in the course of a day, you often find yourself in the same situations more than once. List some of these situations and then describe opportunities in these situations for explaining procedures to patients or your internal customers.

_____

_____

_____

_____

_____

_____

RULE 5: ANTICIPATE NEEDS

You'll often know what people want before they have to ask. Do not wait. Act.

You do not need to be psychic to know when someone needs help. You know so much about your customers' needs because you meet their needs day in and day out. Anticipation is about the little things, the small touches that let patients and other customers know that you understand how they feel and that you want them to feel more comfortable. Examples include:

- Remembering to offer a blanket when you know the patient must wait in a wheelchair or on a stretcher in a cold area.
- Providing an extra pillow to help make the patient feel more comfortable.
- Offering over the phone to send a map to your office when a patient makes an appointment.
- Offering a family member a more comfortable chair or a snack when you notice that he or she is not leaving the patient's bedside.
- Showing an outpatient where the rest room is after he or she has registered.

- Offering a physician a place to do dictation when you see that all the dictation areas are filled.

The fact is that most people do not feel comfortable asking for help. If you offer it without making it necessary for them to ask, they feel impressed and grateful. You help people feel they are not alone—that somebody recognizes their needs. This helps them to understand that others before them have felt the same way in similar situations, which is important because people often feel ashamed of being frightened or awkward, and of not knowing what to expect. By your helpful actions you let people know that there is nothing to feel ashamed of and that you and others in your organization are available to help—even without being asked.

There are many opportunities for you to show your recognition of people's needs and your eagerness to make their lives easier. The following exercise should help you think of a few.

Anticipating Opportunities to be Helpful

List several customers' needs that you could act to address before your customers have to ask. Hint: Start by listing the questions or needs that many of your customers have expressed to you. Can you then do something to meet those needs BEFORE the customer has to express them?

RULE 6: RESPECT PEOPLE'S TIME AND RESPOND QUICKLY

When patients are worried or sick every minute seems like an hour. When co-workers need information or help they find delays frustrating.

Remember the analogy of the hotel guest? In a hotel setting things go along at a leisurely pace. Many people go on vacation to relax, to forget their problems. In a health care setting people are much more likely to feel a sense of urgency and anxiety. People want answers *now*. They want test results *now*. They do not want to have to wait—for their doctor, for news about a loved one, for a conclusive diagnosis, for directions about what to do next, or for that chart or that pill or that answer to their question.

However, a lot of what patients do when they come to see us or order home care is wait—wait for service, wait to be examined, wait for test results. Therefore, it is to our advantage, as well as to theirs, to be sensitive to their needs and considerate of their time.

Nobody likes to wait for service. That is as true in a health care setting as it is in a supermarket checkout line. However, though we are concerned and aware that patients do not like to wait, emergencies do come up and other unexpected interruptions intervene to mess up even the most workable schedule. At times like these, extending goodwill to anxious patients can pay big dividends in return visits and patient loyalty.

When long waits are built into the service a patient is getting, make sure you tell them this up front, along with the reasons for the wait. A typical wait in a large hospital emergency room is several hours. This is agonizing to patients and their families unless the caregivers explain with some degree of thoroughness why the delays are necessary (while they wait for test results, monitor the patient, and more). If they know they will need to wait and if they know approximately how long, they can adjust to this.

When delays involve co-workers or colleagues in another health care setting, alerting them to the delay and the reasons for it is just as important as it is with patients. Perhaps you promised an immediate answer to your colleague's question and you are late in providing it.

Maybe you said you would provide a complete chart or report by a certain deadline and you are going to miss it. Take the initiative to tell them about the delay, apologize for it, and explain.
If delays are not expected, you can also help customers endure them. Here are some suggestions for handling unexpected delays:

- When the physician or other caregiver is detained, explain the reason simply and briefly, and tell the people waiting approximately how long the wait will be. If you know in advance that there will be a wait, try to reach the person before they leave to come to their appointment. This will show your respect for their time much more than telling them upon their arrival—when they can no longer use their time productively.

- Be sure patients and family members are as comfortable as possible during long waits.
- When the wait will be lengthy, give the people options—to go out and run a few errands, to make a call, to get a cup of tea—without losing their places in line.
- A delay on your part may make your patients or other customers late for other appointments and meetings. Make a phone available to them so that they can let others know they're running late. Or offer to make the calls for them.
- Remind your colleagues how long the customer has been waiting so that the caregiver can apologize for the delay and offer an explanation.

When Do You Keep Customers Waiting?

List below the circumstances in which your customers end up waiting longer than they expected. Next to each, jot down good statements you can use to apologize for the delay, explain it, and tell people what they can expect.

SITUATION - WHAT I CAN SAY TO SHOW RESPECT FOR PEOPLE'S TIME

1. _____
2. _____
3. _____

RULE 7: MAINTAIN PRIVACY AND CONFIDENTIALITY

Knock as you enter a patient's room. Watch what you say and where you say it. Protect personal information.

Maintaining the patient's privacy and confidentiality ought to be second nature in a health care setting, where activities as well as information can be sensitive. But this is not always true. Some caregivers deal with sensitive procedures and sensitive information so often that it is commonplace to them. They forget how self-conscious patients feel and how intensely personal they want the experience to remain.

Regarding confidentiality of information, remember that the patient's health information—his or her health status, history, medications, weight, family members—everything related to his or her health, health records and relationships—belongs not to the organization but to the patient. This information is literally about his or her life—body and mind—and what could be more personal and private than that! Every patient has a right to expect confidentiality. When you interview a patient, be sure the setting is private. If you are working in a busy waiting room with no private space available, talk in muted tones and maintain close eye contact with the patient.

Do not carry on conversations about patients with co-workers on crowded elevators or in crowded corridors. You never know who else may be listening nearby. If a co-worker speaks inappropriately about a patient in a public area, whether they are addressing you or not, have the courage to suggest "Why don't we talk further about this in private?"

While patients' health status, friends and family are their private concern, so too is information about your co-workers—their performance problems, salaries, relationships, health status and other personal information are not appropriate news for the grapevine. Share confidential facts about patients, physicians and co-workers only with those whose jobs require access to such information.

Many written communications also need to be kept confidential. Be careful where you place sensitive papers, such as patient charts, personnel paperwork, office notes, and laboratory reports. The next

Patient who sits by your desk may be your last patient's next-door neighbor.

People also deserve your help in protecting their privacy. In hospitals, doctors' offices, nursing homes, and outpatient centers—and also in the patient's home—the patient's room (whichever room the patient is in) belongs to the patient for as long as he or she occupies it. That means that when you enter you should do so as though you were entering someone's private living quarters. Knock before you enter.

Generally, people do not like strangers intruding on their space without advance warning and an explanation about what they are doing there and how long they will be. A badge or a uniform that identifies you as a nurse, an aide, a maintenance worker, or whatever is not sufficient to explain why you have stopped by. Introduce yourself with your name and a friendly greeting, and tell the person why you are there. You need not carry on a complete conversation with the person while you are working. Many patients would find that intrusive. But a courteous introduction and a brief explanation for your visit will help the patient feel at ease—and a little less frightened.

The requirement to knock before entering applies equally to examination rooms. Patients very often feel uncomfortable when they are asked to disrobe for an examination and wait for the physician or nurse. To simply walk in on a person in that situation would be rude and embarrassing.

The following examples of conversations illustrate how you can protect privacy and confidentiality and show respect for the people involved:

- "This is Ms. Colbert, the doctor's assistant. May I come in? I want to ask you some questions."

- "Would you mind if we discussed this in private? I think there's an empty office nearby. I'm concerned that others may overhear us."

- "I'd really like to discuss your father's condition with you in greater detail, Mrs. Harris, but I'm afraid the lobby is too crowded right now for much privacy. Let's see if we can find a better place."

Privacy and confidentiality go hand in hand, but many opportunities for indiscreet behavior arise in a health care setting. Become sensitive to the little things you may do or fail to do that can be interpreted by patients and other customers as an invasion of their privacy or a violation of their right to confidentiality. Complete the exercise below to strengthen your awareness of privacy and confidentiality issues.

Privacy and Confidentiality
Imagine yourself in your customers' situations and think about violations of confidentiality that you would resent. List as many as you can and then identify their remedies.

_____
_____
_____
_____
_____
_____

RULE 8: HANDLE WITH CARE
Slow down. Imagine that you are on the receiving end.

Health care workers often rush from place to place and from patient to patient. Patients and their loved ones may sometimes feel as though they are being treated harshly because of our matter-of-fact tone of voice or gruff handling. Giving a patient a fast ride on a stretcher, quickly lifting and turning a patient, and slamming things down on a patient's bedside table are actions you might do without thinking—a matter of routine. But patients may interpret speed and matter-of-fact handling as roughness. Customers conclude that we are in such a rush to get things done that we forget about their needs and comfort.

When you come in physical contact with patients, it is very important to slow down and show care in the quality of your touch. As you move patients from place to place, imagine the view from their perspective and take steps to help them feel secure and safe in your compassionate hands. Comforting words and gestures such as these go a long way in patient care:

- "I hope my hands aren't too cold."

- "I know you're in pain. I'll be very gentle."

- "Is there anything I can do to make you more comfortable?"

Gentle handling is also important with your co-workers and may include sensitivity to their family problems, to their exhaustion during a rough week, or to their anxiety over a meeting they are about to attend. By providing a calming and soothing presence you can contribute to the feelings of well-being and safety people have in your presence.

Gentle Handling
List below three situations when your customers are under extreme stress and would no doubt appreciate gentle handling. For each situation, list key things you can do to be gentle and show you care.

STRESSFUL SITUATIONS FOR YOUR CUSTOMERS
HOW YOU CAN SHOW YOU CARE

RULE 9: MAINTAIN DIGNITY

Give choices in interactions with patients. Close curtains to provide privacy. That patient could be your child, your partner, your parent or your friend.

All too often in our busy world, helping people takes second place to handling paperwork, following routines, and getting the job done. We have all been in situations in which we felt as though we were treated as nothing more than a number, a case, or maybe even a diagnosis. In health care perhaps more than anywhere else, it is crucial to recognize the individuality and dignity of each of our customers.

Your manner, words and actions show patients and their loved ones that you consider them to be people worthy of your respect. You see lots of customers in any working day, but in many cases each customer sees you only once. Make each customer feel important. Learn customers' names quickly, and use them often. If you have other work to do, put it aside promptly. If you are really pressed for time, explain the situation to the customers and let them know you will finish the other task as quickly as possible and return immediately. That means controlling the volume of your voice, choosing words that are respectful to your customer, and avoiding condescending or patronizing behavior at all costs.

Take action to help the patient feel respected, in an atmosphere where people often feel robbed of their dignity. For example, you might say:

- "Let me get you a robe so you're well covered."

- "Where would you like to sit? On the exam table? Or would you prefer this chair?"

- "So tell me, Mr. Gordon, what kind of work did you do before you retired?"

- Ms. Hoffman, would you mind waiting outside while I help Mrs. Malone?"

When Is Dignity Threatened?
In your role, what things do you do that have the potential to interfere with your customers' dignity? List them below and next to each, write

down a remedy.

**SITUATIONS THAT COULD HURT MY CUSTOMERS' DIGNITY
REMEDIES WITHIN MY POWER**

1. _____
_____
_____

2. _____
_____
_____

3. _____
_____
_____

RULE 10: TAKE THE INITIATIVE

Just because something is not your job does not mean you can't help or find someone who can.
When the problem at hand is not your responsibility or the patient in need is not your patient, act on behalf of the organization anyway. Do what you can for the customer or locate the person who can help so that the customer only has to ask for help *once*.

Remember, sometimes people feel helped because we provided exactly what they wanted—our service, an answer to a question, our advice or directions. Sometimes people feel helped because we listened to them with patience and concern when they were troubled, hurt, frustrated or anxious. And sometimes people feel helped— even if we were not of any direct help at all—because we found the right person to help them in what seemed like a maze of personnel and services.

Perhaps you encountered someone trying to maneuver a wheelchair through a door or into an elevator and you rushed ahead to help out. Or perhaps a co-worker dropped an armful of mail and you volunteered to help carry it. There are many important things that need to be done that are not in anyone's job description—picking up litter, opening doors, cleaning up a spill, giving someone directions. If people do not do these things because it's not their job to, then the burden falls heavily on a small number of good Samaritans. If everyone did his or her share of such things, they would be no great burden on any of us. And important things would get done more quickly and more often, without reliance on red tape or management action.

Taking the initiative to help out when you see that someone has a problem or question only takes a few moments away from the work you are doing, but it pays big dividends in customer satisfaction. And it lets your organization's customers know that you and your co-workers function together as a team and that people are not too busy, too self-centered, or too concerned with their own "turf" to help others in a moment of need.

What's "Not Your Job" and How Can You Act Like It Is?

What situations do you see that trigger the thought "It's not my job!" Next to each, write down a way you could take initiative in this situation so that the situation would not frustrate your customer or you.

"IT'S NOT MY JOB" SITUATIONS   **INITIATIVES I COULD TAKE**

1. _____

_____

_____

2. _____

_____

_____

3. _____

_____

_____

RULE 11: TREAT PATIENTS AS ADULTS

Your words and tone should show respect and consideration.

Being a patient or a patient's loved one often means feeling uncomfortable, helpless and dependent.

Counteract this tendency by respecting your customers' intelligence and maturity.
What do patients perceive as condescending or patronizing behavior on

the part of health care staff?

- When we talk around the patient by directing questions and information meant for the patient to others in the room.
- When we make customers feel stupid for a question they asked.
- When we use the editorial "we" ("Are we ready for our bath?").
- When we use words that relate to children when we're talking to an adult (to an 85-year-old man, "Have you been a good boy since I saw you last?").
- When we use terms we think are endearing instead of people's names ("sweetheart," "darling," "dear," "honey").
- When we raise our voices to an older person because we assume this person is hard of hearing.
- When we respond to a person's feelings in a patronizing tone or with discounting words (as the patient yelps in pain, "Now, now, dear. That didn't hurt at all!").

What may seem like a small matter to you may be of monumental importance to the patient. You may recognize a simple solution to the problem, but as long as they think that the problem is important, it is important. In dealing with people and their needs, showing understanding and respecting the sincerity of their feelings are often more important than solving their problems.

Addressing people by name is a very basic gesture of respect. Patients say that they feel offended when hospital personnel address them in ways they perceive to be inappropriate or demeaning. It is not because we mean to offend but because these familiar forms of address somehow seem easier than learning patients' names.

Here are a few guidelines for addressing customers in a professional manner.

- Address patients and visitors by Mr., Mrs., Miss, or Ms. and their last name first. Then, ask the person what he or she *prefers* to be called. And use their preferred name from then on.

- Don't slip into calling patients "honey," "sweetie," "dear," or" doll." Some people don't mind such familiar terms, but many people do. Why risk offending anyone? Be especially aware of this in your care of older people.

- Start by referring to the person in the most respectful way possible. If you are invited to call a person by his or her first name, consider the invitation a compliment and do so. When in doubt, ask your customers what they prefer to be called.

GUILTY OR NOT GUILTY?

Which of these words do you sometimes use to address a customer?

☐ **Honey or Hon** ☐ **Sweetheart**

☐ **Darling**   ☐ **Sweetie**

☐ **Dear**   ☐ **First names before the customer invites it**

☐ **Doll**   ☐ **Others** _____ _

What can you do to learn people's names so you can avoid these well intentioned but often insulting terms?

When offering information to patients or their loved ones, avoid using technical language or jargon that only your co-workers can understand. Many of your customers do not have your knowledge of health care terminology. What seems easily understandable to you may confuse patients and their family members. Attempt to communicate clearly in terms the customer can understand. On the other hand, avoid talking down to people. Invite questions and be sure the customer understands what you have said before your interaction ends. Unanswered or poorly answered questions leave people anxious and even suspicious about the organization's commitment to meeting their needs.

People are able to read how other people feel toward them. Insincerity can be sensed behind a false smile or an overly enthusiastic tone of voice that tries to convey warmth but only expresses indifference. On the other hand, people respond positively to signs of respect—simple courtesies such as being called by name, being listened to patiently, or being treated with respect.

It's important to demonstrate your respect for your customers by your choice of words and tone of voice. For example:

- "Please let me know if you would like me to repeat or clarify anything, or to speak louder or softer." Suggesting this is far better than assuming that the patient has a hearing problem and speaking in an extremely loud voice.

- "Please ask all the questions you have. I want to be sure that I've been clear and thorough and that you feel clear about everything I've told you today." Using this method ensures that the patient has understood the information you've provided.

Invite Feedback from a Co-Worker

Because your co-workers overhear your interactions with customers day in and day out, perhaps they notice ways you could improve the degree to which your behavior shows respect for customers as adults. Ask them:

1. **What do I do that you think might make my customers feel that I'm not treating them as adults? What signs do you see?**
2. **What do you suggest I can do to help my customers feel respected?**

RULE 12: LISTEN AND ACT

When people complain, do not blame others or make excuses. Hear them out, express your sincere regret that they had a negative experience and then do all you can to respond to the problem and make things right.

Most customers never speak up about problems. Instead, they go away mad and they tell their friends and family how you wronged them. So, bless the dissatisfied customer who speaks up. The more you encourage your customers to speak up, the more loyal they are likely to be to your organization—especially if you can correct the matter and be empathetic in the process.

In the service sector the process of making things right in the face of complaints is known as *service recovery.* In plain language, this means doing all you can to correct a wrong perceived by a customer—and doing it in such a way that the customer's interests are protected and his or her emotions calmed.

If you are feeling resistant right now, you aren't alone. Many health care workers resist gracious, energetic, resourceful handling of complaints for five reasons:

- Some people don't believe in apologizing; they feel that by apologizing, they are admitting a mistake. But the magic words "I'm sorry" help people know that you sincerely regret that they've had a negative experience.

- Some are annoyed by what they believe are excessively high expectations on the part of the customer. They don't think the customer should be angry, because he or she "wants the impossible."

- Some people don't know how to respond graciously, so the situation leaves them feeling uncomfortable or embarrassed.

- Some want to make things right, but they can't make things right by themselves. They don't have the power to do so without others' help. And they feel that they can't depend on getting that help

- Some want to make things right, but don't know who to turn to when red tape must be cut or other decisions made in order to do so.

While these reasons have a grain of truth, they are no excuse for defensive responses to customer complaints. The best medicine for handling distraught or upset patients, family members, physicians, insurers and co-workers, no matter how much or how little power you have to take concrete action, is letting them talk out their frustrations—but without getting upset yourself! Don't hesitate to say, "I'm sorry you had that experience." Or, "I'm so sorry it's been frustrating for you." Then, acknowledge the persons feelings and ask for information so you can figure out what to do. By acknowledging the person's feelings and inviting them to explain further, you will have a calming effect and gain information key to finding a solution to the problem at hand.

Anger often camouflages other emotions. It covers up deeper feelings that cannot get out until the anger has been expressed. Anger hides fear, rejection, insecurity, frustration, disappointment, and a host of other feelings. By allowing your customer to blow off steam you can get to the emotions behind the anger, and that will put you in a position to understand and help. Help the anger to come out, and you will see the person's real feelings come through—and you will open the possibility of reaching a solution or at least a new understanding.

While it is critical to listen and allow your customers to get their feelings out into the open, it is also important to know when to stop an interaction. When an emotionally charged interaction is allowed to drag on past its resolution, it loses its effectiveness. Once the problem has been resolved or you have done all you can under the circumstances, you should courteously and tactfully end the contact.

Good listeners are not born; they are made. You can learn to be a good listener with a little practice and attention to the following tips:

- **Listen with purpose.** Ask yourself what it is you want to find out and what it is you expect or want to hear. What might the speaker say that will affect your preconceived ideas or plans?

- **Listen for meaning.** There are several levels on which people communicate. There are the words themselves and the implications behind the words—nuance and tone of voice. There are also nonverbal cues—posture, facial expression, gestures, and so forth. It is important to listen with your eyes as well as your ears, to listen for what is not said but felt.

- **Eliminate distractions.** Whenever possible you should give your undivided attention to the speaker. You want the speaker to have the opportunity to express himself or herself without distractions.

- **Don't jump in.** Try not to reply too quickly. Instead, briefly restate what you heard to make sure you understood it. Then, formulate your reply and respond. Even though you think quickly and may already have a response in mind, it pays to listen until the other person has finished so that you don't miss anything.

- **Be an active listener.** Involve yourself in the listening process. Be aware of your own listening barriers and guard against them. Take the time to become aware of your thoughts and reactions.

- **Take notes and check for understanding**. If the concerns are numerous or involved, tell the customer that you would like to jot down key points so you can follow through without forgetting anything. This gives the complainer confidence that you care and also makes it easier for you to find the people or resources you'll need to take whatever corrective actions are possible.

When a Customer Complains:

1. Listen without interruption.
2. Don't get defensive.
3. Use a "sad, but glad" statement ("I'm sorry you've been inconvenienced, but I'm very glad you're bringing it to my attention).
4. Express empathy ("I can certainly see how upsetting this was!").
5. Ask questions to clarify the problem.
6. Find out what the customer wants.
7. Explain what you can and cannot do.
8. Discuss the alternatives fully.
9. Take action.
10. Follow up to ensure customer satisfaction

By being an attentive and sensitive listener, you let people know that you care. You show that your customers' concerns matter to you. Let them tell you what is on their minds, and do not be defensive. Then take whatever actions you can to make things right.

Devoting time and effort to building your skills in complaint handling or service recovery will not only pay off in greater customer satisfaction but also give you the tools you need to calm angry customers, thus reducing the stress on you. The following steps constitute an effective process for handling complaints skillfully—a process that can indeed be learned!

Effective handling of complaints starts with a positive, welcoming attitude toward them. If we were wise, we would actually beg customers to complain. After all, if complaints are not voiced, we cannot fix them. And customers go away, taking their feelings of resentment with them—and their business elsewhere.

Important Times to Listen
You know your customers and your work. List below three situations in which your customers show signs of dissatisfaction or frustration. Next to each, write down words you could use to acknowledge their feelings and invite them to express their feelings and concerns.

SITUATIONS THAT FRUSTRATE CUSTOMERS - HOW I CAN INVITE THEM TO SPEAK UP

1. _____

_____

_____

2. _____

_____

_____

3. _____

_____

_____

RULE 13: HELP EACH OTHER

When you help your co-workers, you help patients too.

Positive co-worker relationships—teamwork and cooperation—are critical to the smooth operation of any organization. The way staff members interact can color the customer's image of you, your team and your organization. A harmoniously cooperative staff builds confidence among patients and their loved ones. A quick-to-help staff makes physicians choose your organization over others. And harmonious co-worker relationships reduce the stress that is a daily fact in the lives of health care professionals today.

Here are a few tips on improving the quality of your work relationships for the sake of patients. Please note that these tips also improve the quality of your work life and relationships.

- Cooperation is contagious. Give it and you'll receive it.

- Every job is unique. Take care of yours, and let others take care of theirs. We're not here to judge.

- If you have criticisms, keep them constructive. Speak directly to the source of the problem. Gossiping about a difficult situation or person won't make it or them go away.

- Avoid negativism. It drains you and depletes others.

- Build supportive relationships—everyone performing stressful jobs needs them.

- Be generous in expressing appreciation. It pays great dividends.

- Look and act the part of a professional. Your professional demeanor or lack of it reflects on your colleagues, affecting the respect customers have for all of you as professionals.

- Be careful not to interrupt others when it's not really necessary. Interruptions distract your co-workers and, at times, make them feel inefficient, irritable and tense.

- Help your co-workers to like themselves. Be genuinely interested in others and get them to talk about themselves. Ask for their opinions, ideas and viewpoints.

- Be a role model. Make your service a better and more respected service because you're in it.

Some people think that their behavior toward customers is all that matters, that they can show their true feelings toward co-workers. But the fact is that customers draw conclusions about your team's competence, compassion and ability to work together as a team by reading your behavior toward one another.

- One nurse says to the other in front of a patient, "I'm sick and tired of covering for you when you're late."

- A physician says to the billing clerk, "Can't you get this right?!"

- One staff member whispers within earshot of visitors, "Can you believe, he's got a crush on that patient!"

- In front of a patient, the nurse asks the student, "Is this your first time doing this procedure?"

- One caregiver says to another, "I am not going to cover your patient. I have more patients than you and I've been running ragged all morning while you've talked on the phone!"

Patients and families are sensitive people who can draw conclusions from what they overhear even if it is not directed at them. They can detect tension in the air. Interpersonal differences among co-workers negatively affect the customer's comfort and sense of security and leave people wondering "If you can't take care of yourselves, how can you take care of us?" You lose their trust. Let your differences take a back seat to the care you are giving to your customers, and if necessary, seek a third party's advice on settling differences.

Look for ways to help your co-workers make their own jobs run more smoothly. When convenient, answer their phones while they are otherwise occupied. Offer to mail a package for them when you are going in that direction. Take the initiative and anticipate your co-workers' needs for help, cooperation and support

Ask yourself:

1. What *drives you crazy about your co-workers?*
2. *What probably drives them crazy about you?*
3. *Looking at your answers to 1 and 2 above, commit yourself to three "do's" and three "don'ts" that will help you to improve your relationships with your co-workers and, as a result, improve the teamwork and harmony you help to create among your work team and in front of customers.*

_____

_____

_____

RULE 14: KEEP IT QUIET

Noise annoys. It also shows a lack of consideration and concern for patients, co-workers and your other customers.

We are all familiar with signs that say "Quiet—Hospital Zone." Usually these signs are outside the hospital and apply to motor vehicles. But the noise that is generated inside any health care facility's walls, whether it is a hospital, clinic, doctor's office or diagnostic facility, distracts and annoys patients more than any noise from outside.

Research has shown that noise levels in health care facilities are so extreme that they can cause adverse health outcomes for patients and reduce staff productivity. It is not exclusively machinery, squeaky carts and equipment noise that causes strain. People noise—normal conversations, loud talking, yelling down the hall, heavy footsteps and so on—contributes significantly to the problem.

Patients and staff can usually accept the necessary noises of a health care organization—cleaning equipment, delivery carts, moderated talk, etc. But they resent unnecessary noise that makes resting impossible for patients and concentrating difficult for staff. Unnecessary noise includes loud talking, boisterous laughing, doors banging, and so on.

Furthermore, noise that is appropriate in hospitals and nursing homes during the day may not be appropriate at night. People expect respectful quiet during the evening and until 8:00 or 9:00 in the morning. Patients greatly resent being awakened by unchecked voices and loud laughter.

Generally speaking, special care is needed in the following sensitive areas:

- In and near the intensive care unit, cardiac care unit, and operating room.
- Near people on stretchers.
- Near resting or distressed patients in elevators, halls and waiting areas.
- In patient care and patient living areas of all kinds—patient rooms, exam and treatment rooms, and the like.

To do your part to keep the noise down, consider these simple guidelines:

- Be aware of how loud, how long, and when you talk. Make a conscious effort to control the noise associated with your conversations.
- Hold your conversations where appropriate. Ask yourself whether your conversation is appropriate in the elevator, outside a patient's

room, or near a congested nurses' station or front desk.

- Avoid calling out, yelling down the hall, or shouting. Get reasonably close to the person you're talking to so that you don't have to raise your voice.

- See whether you can move, place, open, close, pull, push, put down, roll, wheel, and slide things more quietly. Carry around oil can if you interact with lots of equipment daily.

- Take extra pains to avoid making banging, bumping, slamming, dropping and rattling noises.

- Adjust the volume of your voice according to where you are in the hospital.

- Have the guts to be a "quiet advocate." Say to people you're with, "I think we're getting too loud." Or on the elevator, "Let's talk about this somewhere else." Or "Maybe we shouldn't talk here. I'm concerned that we're too close to the patient's room.

- Be sure to answer your telephone quickly. When possible, keep the volume of the telephone chime turned down low.

If you have doubts about the therapeutic value of keeping the noise down, here is a brief rundown of some of the things that noise does to patients:

- Increases perception of pain.

- Interferes with sleep.

- Leads to irritability and anxiety.

- Triggers high blood pressure, a major cause of strokes and heart attacks.

- Is interpreted as an insult.

And here is what noise does to you and your co-workers:

- Creates stress, a major cause of illness.

- Makes people irritable and argumentative.

- Makes people lose patience.

- Reduces concentration and problem-solving ability.
- Makes people less sociable and more aggressive.
- Promotes accidents and mistakes.
- Makes it very hard to be sensitive to the needs of others.

Do a Noise Audit

1. Convene your work team and ask "What are all the noises our customers hear when they're here?" Make a long list and then ask yourselves, "Which of these are within our control? Which can we reduce?" Do some problem-solving and commit to some noise reduction remedies.

   _____

   _____

   _____

   _____

   _____

   _____

2. Ask your customers to identify noise that bothered them during their time with you. Tell them you're working on ways to reduce the stress patients feel when they come to your facility and that *noise* is one element. They'll be impressed and they'll give you some good information—information about noise that you might have tuned out

   _____

   _____

   _____

   _____

   _____

   _____

Keep the noise down when you can. And if you cannot, explain the source of the noise and how long it will last. This will reduce patients and co-workers' anxiety that results from noises they do not understand or that they expect to continue indefinitely.

RULE 15: APPLY TELEPHONE SKILLS

When you are on the telephone, your organization's reputation is on the line. Sound pleasant, and be helpful. Listen with understanding. Do not be shy about asking a caller to repeat himself or herself on the telephone so that you get all the information you need accurately. If you do not have the answer to a question at your fingertips, ask the caller's permission to put the call on hold, and ask someone who does know. Or, if the answer will take a while to find out, ask the person whether you can call back later. If you must place a caller on hold be sure to check back with the caller frequently.

Often the first encounter a patient or family member has with your organization is by telephone. The success of that encounter can determine whether the customer decides to use your organization or to try another. Here are a few tips to make your telephone contacts good experiences for your customers:

- Before you pick up the telephone, finish your other office conversations.

- Put a smile on your face even before you say hello. Your attitude will come across in your voice.

- Answer promptly—at least by the third ring but preferably on the second—and identify yourself. For example, say: "Good morning, Einstein Practice Plan. Mary Smith. May I help you?"

- Listen attentively to the caller and concentrate on what he or she is saying. If you can't understand what is being said, tactfully say "I'm having difficulty hearing you. Would you mind repeating that?" If you need to consult someone else in the office, be sure to put the caller on hold. Background noises are annoying to the caller and sound unprofessional.

- If you need to get the attention of someone else in the office who is on the telephone, place a written note in front of that person and wait for a response.

- If a caller has reached your extension by mistake, take the time to help find the right number. Transfer the call if you can, and be sure to give the caller the number in case the other line is busy or the call is accidentally disconnected.

GET A TELEPHONE CHECK·UP
Identify three co-workers who call you often. Make copies of the form below and ask them to fill out this form about you the next time they call you, and then return it to you.
TELEPHONE CHECK-UP
Your Name _____ *Observer's Name*

DID I

Sound welcoming and friendly?	DID	SO-SO	NO!
Identify myself with my name?	YES	NO	
Identify my department or organization?	YES	NO	
Respond effectively to your needs as a caller	YES	NO	

What tips can you offer me to help me be more effective with customers on the telephone?

    1._____

    2._____

    3._____

Just as first contacts often take place by telephone, complaints are often registered by telephone. Nobody enjoys handling complaints, but the way in which they are handled can often mean the difference between keeping a customer and losing one.

Remember that complaints are really opportunities—opportunities to know what customers find disagreeable about your organization—and a second chance to make things right. A customer's complaint should not be regarded as a nuisance, but as a valuable suggestion and opportunity to improve service.

Here are a few tips for handling complaints over the telephone:

■ Encourage the speaker to express his or her thoughts completely. Sound calm and interested as you do.

■ Write down important details, phrases and facts.

- Repeat these details to the caller to be sure that you have them right.

- Sympathize with the caller. This has a calming effect.

- Don't lose your cool! Maintain a pleasant tone.

- Tell the caller what you plan to do about the complaint.

- Apologize for the caller's inconvenience or difficulty even when you had nothing to do with it. Don't be defensive. Remember that to the caller you are the organization during the telephone interaction. Therefore, you must act as the whole organization's representative.

RULE 16: LOOK THE PART

Professional dress and demeanor build people's confidence in all of us.

We want people to feel they are in good hands—secure and confident in the people who are taking care of them. The way you look—the way you dress, stand and sit—communicate competence or the lack of it. A desk that looks like a paper jungle or evidence of careless grooming often suggests disorganization or a lack of interest in oneself, and our customers interpret that as a lack of care for them as well.

Professional dress is dress that does not offend or distract but instead identifies us as professionals. Sneakers with holes in them, dangling jewelry, a prominent scent of cologne, tight or revealing clothing—according to what patients tell us—make them wonder about the people they are trusting with their care.

LOOK AT YOURSELF NOW!
Look at how you look today. Ask yourself:

1. **Do I look professional?**
2. **Does my image say, "You're in good hands here"?**

What image issues do I need to pay attention to?

_____

_____

_____

Consider the fact that your appearance tells more about your sense of self-worth and dignity than it does about your bank account. You are part of a long, proud medical tradition, and customers who visit your organization expect you to look the part.

HOW CAN YOU APPLY THE 16 HOUSE RULES?

Putting the 16 House Rules into practice will not turn any health care organization into a posh hotel. But following the rules will make coming to your facility or seeking your services a memorable experience because of the comfort, convenience, consideration and compassion it provides. When these qualities are lacking, even routine health maintenance can become an ordeal that people will not want to repeat, at least not in your hands.

Your organization understands the value of keeping each and every customer and through your practice of the 16 House Rules you will be doing your part to reflect your organization's professional standards of excellence. You will also find that your own work will become more gratifying as you heighten customer satisfaction, and you will reap the rewards that flow from job satisfaction: pride and gratification that you are doing your part on the health care team and promoting excellence in customer service.

Facing the Challenge— From Good to Great

While the 16 House Rules are nothing new or profound, the challenge is twofold. The first challenge is to adhere to the house rules *consistently,* no matter what your workload, your mood, or the behavior of the customer. That is not very easy. It means getting a grip on your negative feelings and circumstances and learning to play the role of the professional in spite of your feelings and circumstances. That is the mark of a true professional. By adhering to these rules consistently no matter how you feel, you will reduce the number of negative incidents with customers—incidents that, although infrequent, nonetheless have a profound influence on customer satisfaction.

The second challenge is to identify and seize opportunities to be *excellent* not just *good* in your interactions with your customers. The public notices extremes in customer service performance. They notice negative offenses, and they notice remarkable, moving, meaningful, positive interactions. Adequate, mediocre or inoffensive behavior tends to go unnoticed. The challenge then is to move from good to great. You must look for the fine points and possibilities in your behavior that would actively impress customers, instead of just failing to offend them.

Here is an example. Imagine a front-desk receptionist who looks up when approached by a customer and says, in a flat although polite tone "Good morning, may I help you?" Not bad. In fact, many employers would be thrilled if every one of their employees greeted every customer at least that well. But that kind of greeting is not excellent. It is adequate, appropriate and professional, but not excellent. The employee has missed opportunities to go the extra steps that would make the customer take notice.

Imagine instead that as the customer approaches the employee stands up, moves toward the customer, extends a hand, and says with a warm smile "Good morning, welcome to Bayside Medical! My name is Sammy Smith. How may I help you?" If you ask customers they will tell you how pleased they are when a front-desk person greets them with a smile, an introduction, and a warm offer to help. That is excellence. The point is, every one of us can move from good to excellent by examining our behavior and incorporating the fine points that make a difference to the customers.

LOOKING IN THE MIRROR

How do you rate on applying the house rules? How often do you adhere to these simple guidelines for behavior? On the following pages, you will find two charts for rating customer service behavior. Use the first to rate your own behavior according to the house rules. Then invite one or more co-workers to share their perceptions of the extent to which you follow the house rules by filling out the second chart. You might do this exercise with several co-workers.

If you are like most of us, even when you have achieved high levels of accomplishment in customer service there is still room for improvement and fine-tuning. Practicing customer service skills with co-workers in staff meetings, in training sessions, and at lunch will allow you to pool the best of all your skills.

RATING YOURSELF!

What's your sense of how often you show the following behaviors? Put a check mark in the appropriate column for how often you exhibit these customer service behaviors.

	RARELY	AT TIMES	OFTEN	ALWAYS	NOT MY JOB
I smile at patients, their loved ones, and co-workers.					
I make eye contact with patients, their loved ones, and co-workers.					
I introduce myself to patients.					
I call people by name.					
I help people who look confused.					
I let patients and guests go first (in elevators, in cafeteria lines, through doors, etc.).					
I explain to patients and co-workers what I'm doing.					
I see what people need and help before having to be asked.					
I respond quickly to patients' needs. I respond quickly to co-					

workers' needs. I knock as I enter a patient's room.					
When I touch or move patients, I handle them gently.					
I protect patients' dignity by covering them and closing their curtains and doors.					
I watch what I say and where I say it, maintaining confidentiality.					
When something is needed that isn't my job, I help anyway or find someone who can					
I treat patients as adults, and my words and tone show it.					
When people complain, I listen don't snap back or make excuses.					
I'm courteous, cooperative, and helpful with co-workers.					
I keep my voice down in halls, at nursing stations, and in and around patient rooms.					
On the telephone, I sound pleasant,					

listen, and go the extra step to be helpful.				
I look professional in dress, grooming and manner.				

What your sense is of how often _____ shows the following behaviors? Put a check mark in the appropriate column for how often _____ exhibits these customer service behaviors.

	RARELY	AT TIMES	OFTEN	ALWAYS	NOT MY JOB
Employee smiles at patients, their loved ones, and co-workers					
Employee makes eye contact with patients, their loved ones, and co-workers.					
Employee introduces himself or herself to patients.					
Employee calls people by name.					
Employee helps people who look on fused.					
Employee lets					

patients and guests go first (in elevators, In cafeteria lines, through doors, etc.).					
Employee explains to patients and co-workers 58 what he or she is doing.					
Employee sees what people needs and helps before having to be asked.					
Employee responds quickly to patients' needs.					
Employee responds quickly to co-workers' needs.					
Employee knocks as he or she enters a patient's room.					
When Employee touches or moves patients, he or she handles them gently.					
Employee protects patients' dignity by covering them and closing their curtains and doors.					

Employee watches what he or she says and where he or she says it, maintaining confidentiality.					
When something is needed that isn't my job, Employee helps anyway or find someone who can.					
Employee treats patients as adults, and his or her words and tone show it.					
When people complain, the employee listen she or she doesn't snap back or make excuses.					
Employee is courteous, cooperative, and helpful with co-workers.					
Employee keeps his or her voice down in halls, at nursing stations, and in and around patient rooms.					
On the telephone, employee					

sounds pleasant, listens, and goes the extra step to be helpful.				
Employee looks professional in dress, grooming and manner.				

Scoring

- If more than 15 of your checks are in the frequently column, you're among the top 5 percent of health care employees in providing consistently professional customer service.

- If most of your checks fall in the columns marked occasionally and hardly ever, you're among friends. That is how most health care employees rate themselves. But that is not excellence! Look for opportunities to fine-tune your customer service effectiveness

- Look over your co-worker's ratings of your behavior. Ask yourself "What differences and similarities are there between my self-ratings and my co-worker's ratings of my behavior?" If you see differences, it might help to look again at your behavior and accept the possibility that you might not be as effective as you think.

- The challenge: Expend the effort and attention needed to bring everyone in your organization up to the level of excellence that would make your customers happy and you proud.

SATISFYING THE CUSTOMER IS EVERYBODY'S BUSINESS

Businesses that are highly successful make customer satisfaction their top priority. Even the best-designed, best-constructed product or service can be lost in a sea of competition if the organization is not outstanding in achieving customer satisfaction. Everything highly successful businesses do, in fact, is aimed solely at satisfying the customer. To accomplish this goal every employee must do whatever possible to provide wonderful service, showing commitment to their customers and to the organization's service mission.

As the poster that follows suggests, in health care, a commitment to providing excellent service carries with it a tremendous responsibility. With that responsibility you have the precious opportunity to contribute to the well-being of other people, acting on your commitment to our important health care mission.

You ARE Your Organization!

- You are what people see when they arrive here.

- Yours are the eyes they look into when they're frightened and anxious, or lonely

- Yours is the voice people hear when they ride the elevators, when they try to rest, and when they try to forget their problems. You are what they hear on their way to appointments that could affect their destinies, and what they hear after they leave those appointments.

- Yours are the comments people hear when you think they can't

- Yours is the intelligence and caring that people hope they'll find here. If you're noisy, so is your organization. If you're rude, so is your organization. And if you're wonderful, so is your Organization

- No visitors, no patients, no physicians or co-workers can ever know the real you, the one that you know is there-unless you let them see it. All they can know is what they see, hear and experience.

And so your organization has a stake in your attitude and in the collective attitudes of everyone who works there. Your entire team is judged by your performance. All are judged by the care you give, the attention you pay, and the courtesies you extend

Thank you for all you are doing.

Best-Selling Books by Wendy Leebov, Ed.D.
http://www.quality-patient-experience.com/wendy-leebov-books.html

Physician Entrepreneurs: The Quality Patient Experience -- Improve outcomes, boost quality scores, and increase revenue *(Book and CD-2008)* Built around the key areas in the CAHPS survey, this book and tool-packed CD offers quick and easy techniques that physicians and practice staff can use to enhance the patient experience—without sacrificing productivity.

Wendy Leebov's Essentials for Great Patient Experiences: No Nonsense Solutions with Gratifying Results *(2008)* Specific tools that enhance the patient experience and address the difficulties staff have in delivering the exemplary care they would like to provide. High-impact strategies for moving your service excellence and patient satisfaction to a new level, resulting in higher scores on HCAHPS and CG-CAHPS.

Wendy Leebov's Essentials for Great Personal Leadership: No Nonsense Solutions with Gratifying Results *(2008)* Valuable problem-solving and leadership development for health care executives, mid-level administrators, department heads, clinical leaders, and anyone who brings a passion to their work. Each chapter captures the essence of emotionally intelligent leadership and focuses on effective solutions.

Service Quality Improvement: The Customer Satisfaction Strategy for Health Care
(Leebov and Scott) A goldmine of approaches for your service excellence initiative, that helps you build a service-oriented culture and focusing all employees on service excellence and continuous service improvement.

The Indispensable Health Care Manager: Success Strategies for a Changing
Environment *(Leebov and Scott - 2003 Health Care Book of the Year)* Identifies ten role shifts needed by managers who want to add significant value to their organizations and enhance their employability. Self-assessments, case situations and concrete tools that build key leadership competencies.

Also by Wendy Leebov—practical guides that help frontline employees provide the exceptional patient and family experience
- Assertiveness Skills for Professionals in Health Care
- Customer Service for Professionals in Health Care
- Telephone Skills for Professionals in Health Care
- Resolving Complaints for Professionals in Health Care
- Working Together for Professionals in Health Care

Enrich Your Tools and Confidently Guide Your Team to the Next Level
http://www.quality-patient-experience.com/wendy-leebov-books.html

23654085R00035

Made in the USA
Middletown, DE
15 December 2018